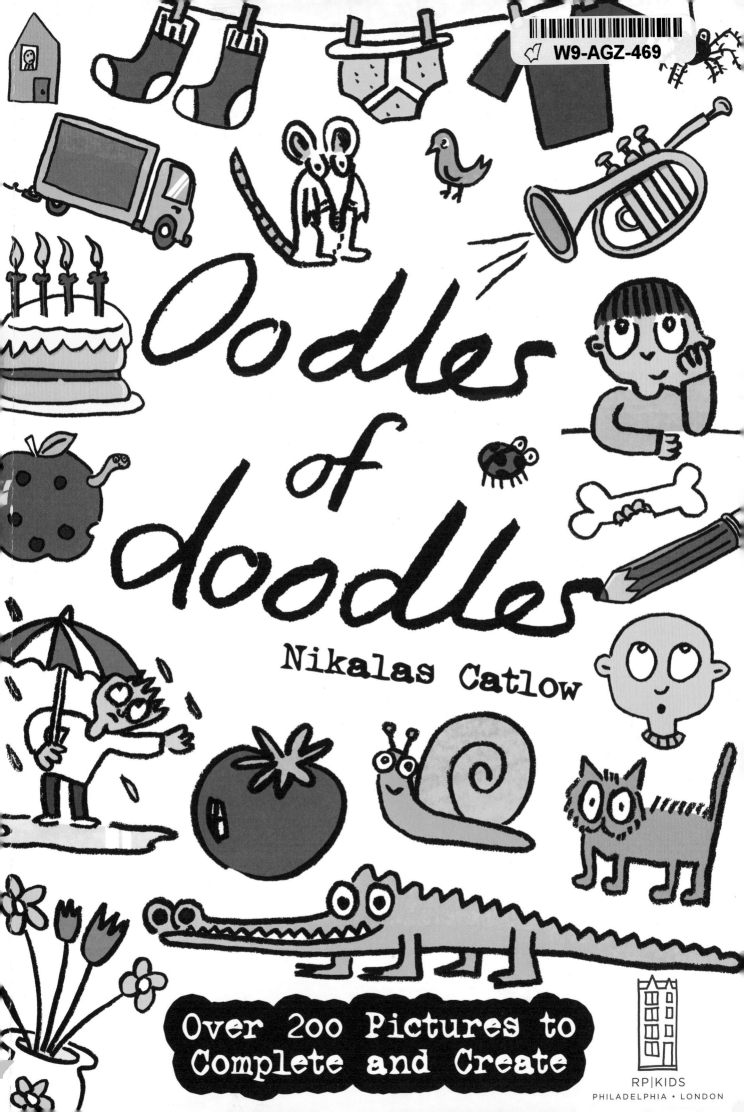

Oodles of doodles

Nikalas Catlow

Over 200 Pictures to Complete and Create

RP|KIDS
PHILADELPHIA • LONDON

Illustrated by Nikalas Catlow for Amy P.

First published in Great Britain in 2008 by Buster Books,
an imprint of Michael O'Mara Books Limited, 9 Lion Yard, Tremadoc Road, London SW4 7NQ.

First published in the United States by Running Press Book Publishers, 2009

Printed in China

Books published by Running Press are available at special discounts for bulk purchases in the United States
by corporations, institutions, and other organizations. For more information, please contact the
Special Markets Department at the Perseus Books Group, 2300 Chestnut Street, Suite 200, Philadelphia,
PA 19103, or call (800) 810-4145, ext. 5000, or e-mail special.markets@perseusbooks.com.

ISBN 978-0-7624-5294-1

9 8 7 6 5 4 3 2 1
Digit on the right indicates the number of this printing

This edition published by:
Running Press Kids
An Imprint of Running Press Book Publishers
A Member of the Perseus Books Group
2300 Chestnut Street
Philadelphia, PA 19103–4371

Visit us on the web!
www.runningpress.com/kids

What's eating the leaves?

Disguise me.

Build a giant burger.

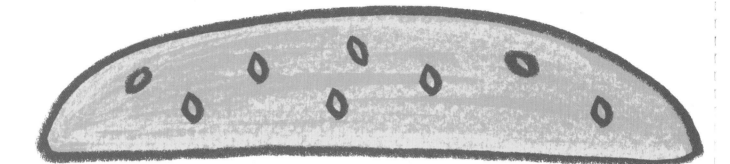

Make the house haunted.

What are elephants
scared of?

What am I chasing?

What's chasing me?

Scary movie...

What is being delivered?

What would you take to a desert island?

What has the dinosaur eaten?

Why is he crying?

Put some worms in the apple.

Give the crown some jewels.

Turn the fountains on.

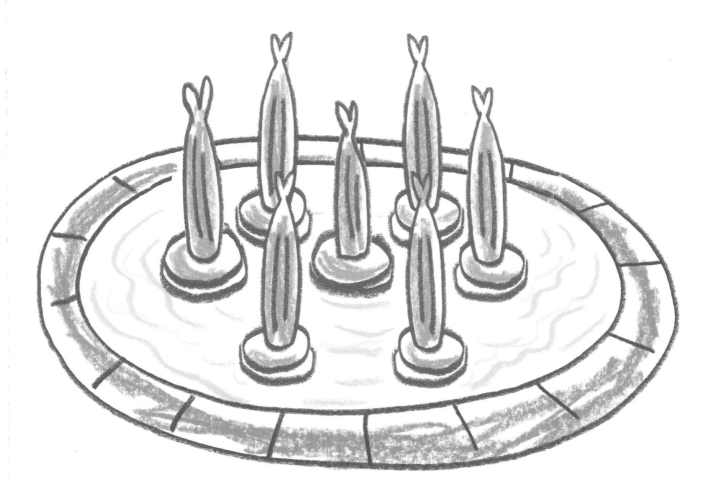

Who's on the train?

Who's on the platform?

A happy thought...

A sad thought...

How tall is a giant?

Make some noise.

Timber!

I'm sick.

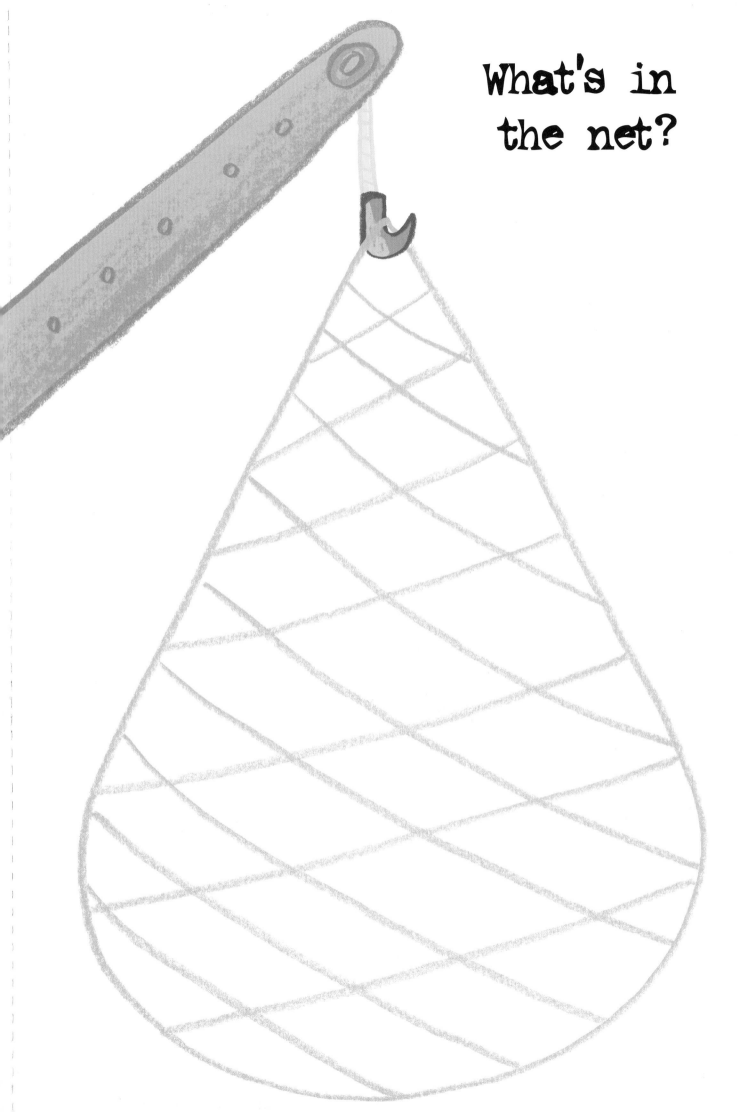

What's in the net?

What's at the end
of the rainbow?

Who's been eating?

I love my pet.

What's through the keyhole?

The animals have escaped from the zoo.

What's in the sack?

Make a forest.

Stack them high.

Rectangular things...

Who's at the party?

What's in the handbag?

Half person, half animal...

Fill the pit.

Whose ears?

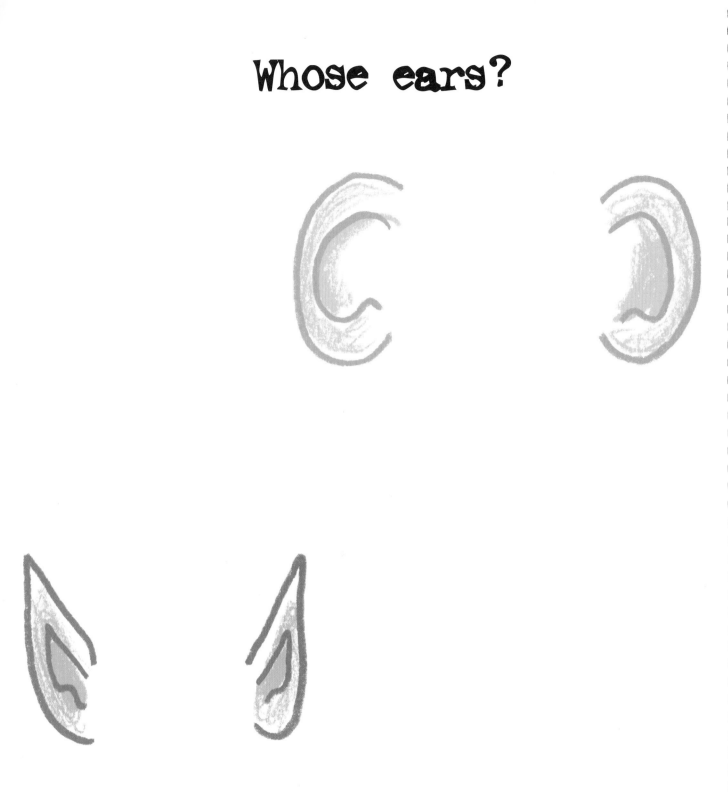

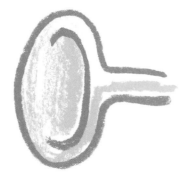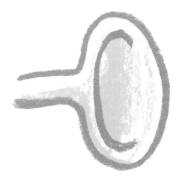

Add windows.

Add more slime.

Finish the machine.

Things I like...

Things I don't like...

What can you see in space?

Jump on the trampoline.

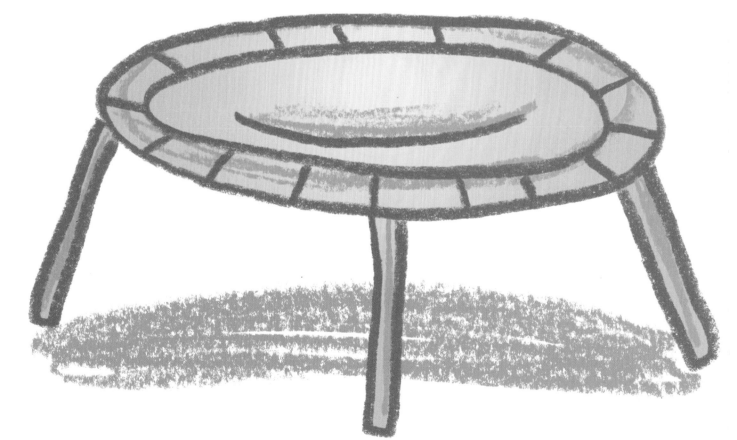

What happens when you press the magic button?

What's hiding in the closet under the stairs?

Make it winter.

The world's silliest haircuts...

The world's strangest creature...

What's the cat catching?

Bungee!

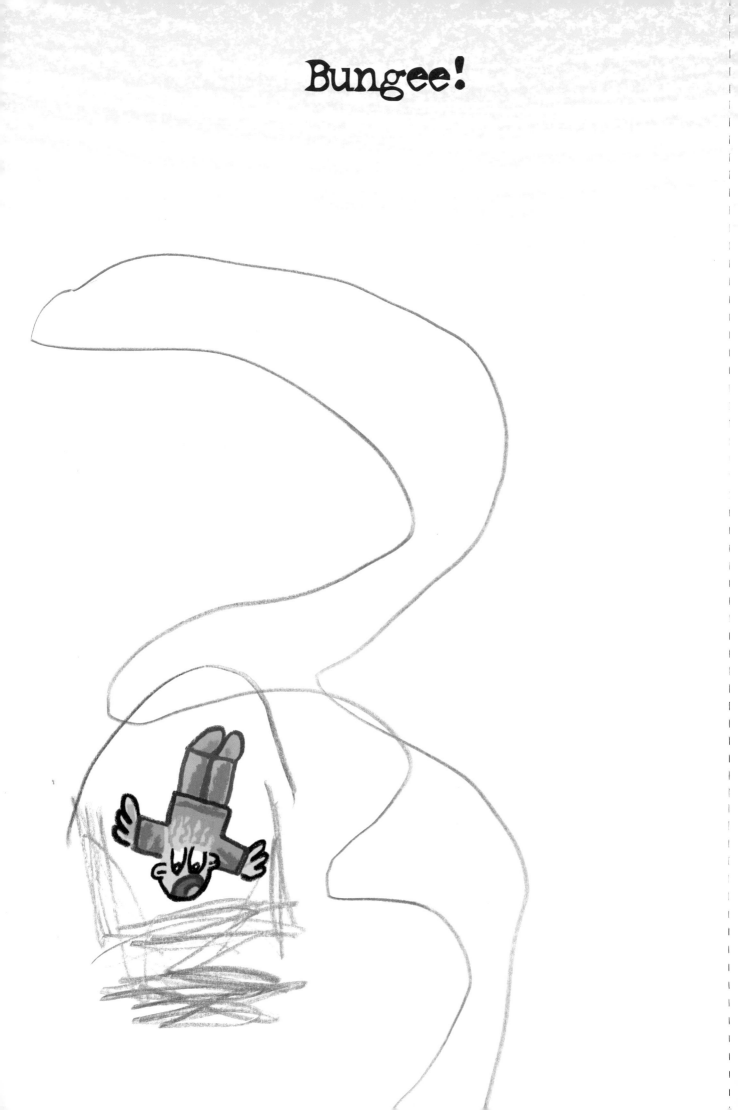

What are you feeding?

What can the dentist see?

What are you controlling?

Who's he following?

Fill the
doll's house.

What makes you laugh?

What's outside the tent?

I'm the king of the castle.

What was that?

Grow some fruit on the tree.

What am I licking?

It came from out of the ground!

happy

sad

angry

tired

confused

ho....y....

The world's longest spaghetti noodle.

Wow! What do they keep in here?

X-ray specs...

It's noisy.

Everyone wants a mustache.

Who's at the pool?

What can you see
under the sea?

I spy with my little eye something beginning with A.

URRGH! What's that?

What's in the
secret drawer?

How many birds
are on the wire?

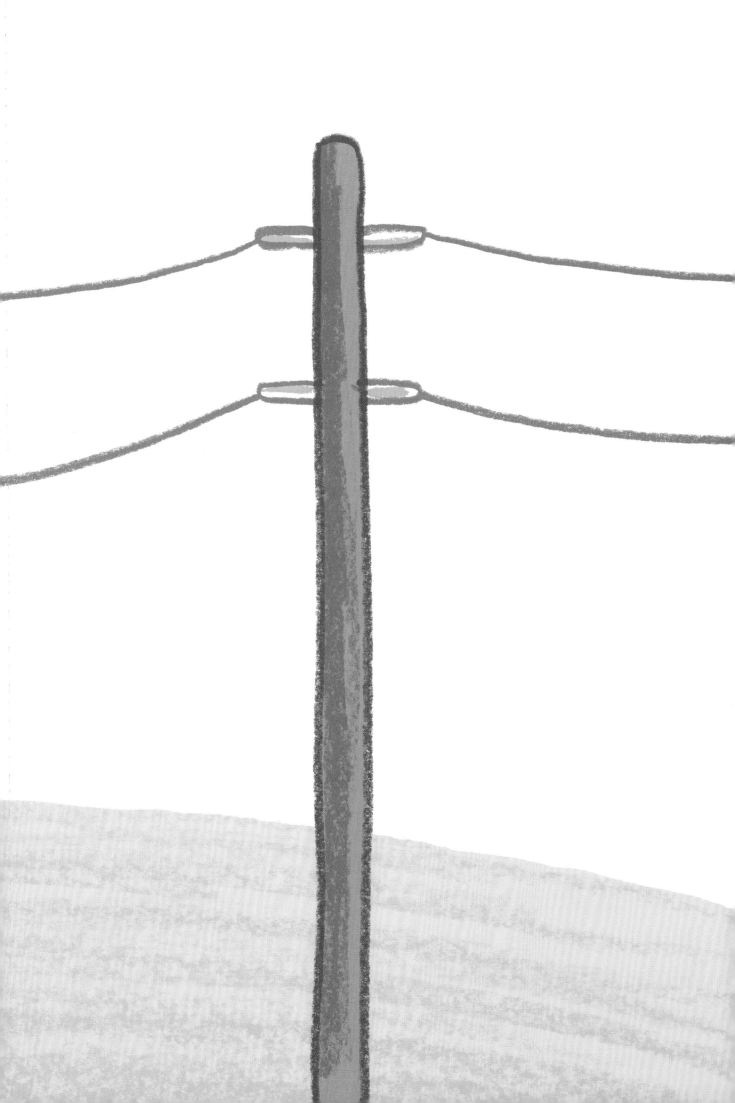

Whose tails are these?

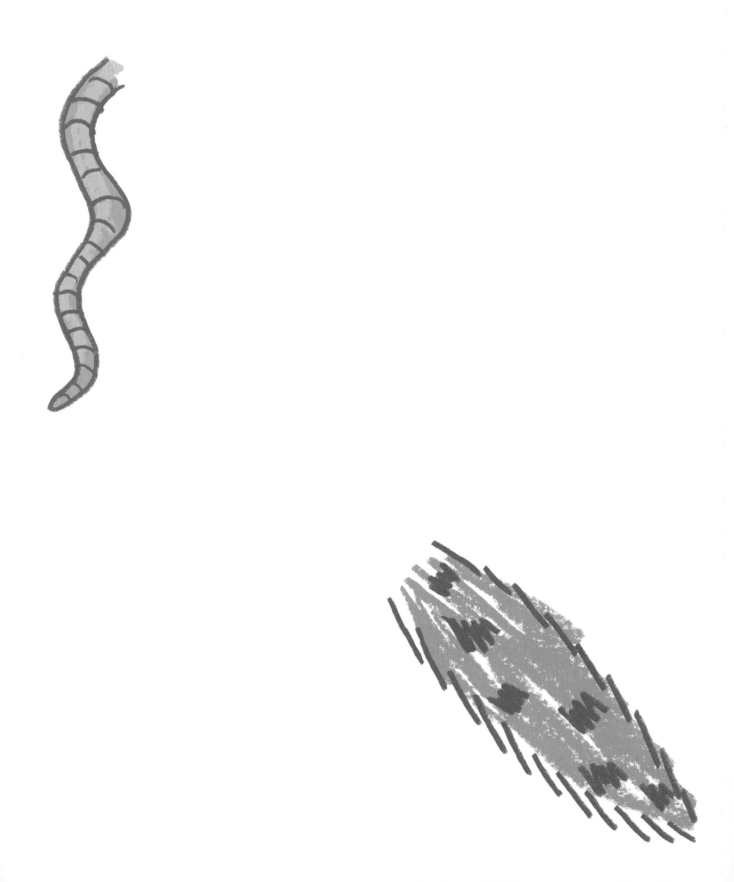

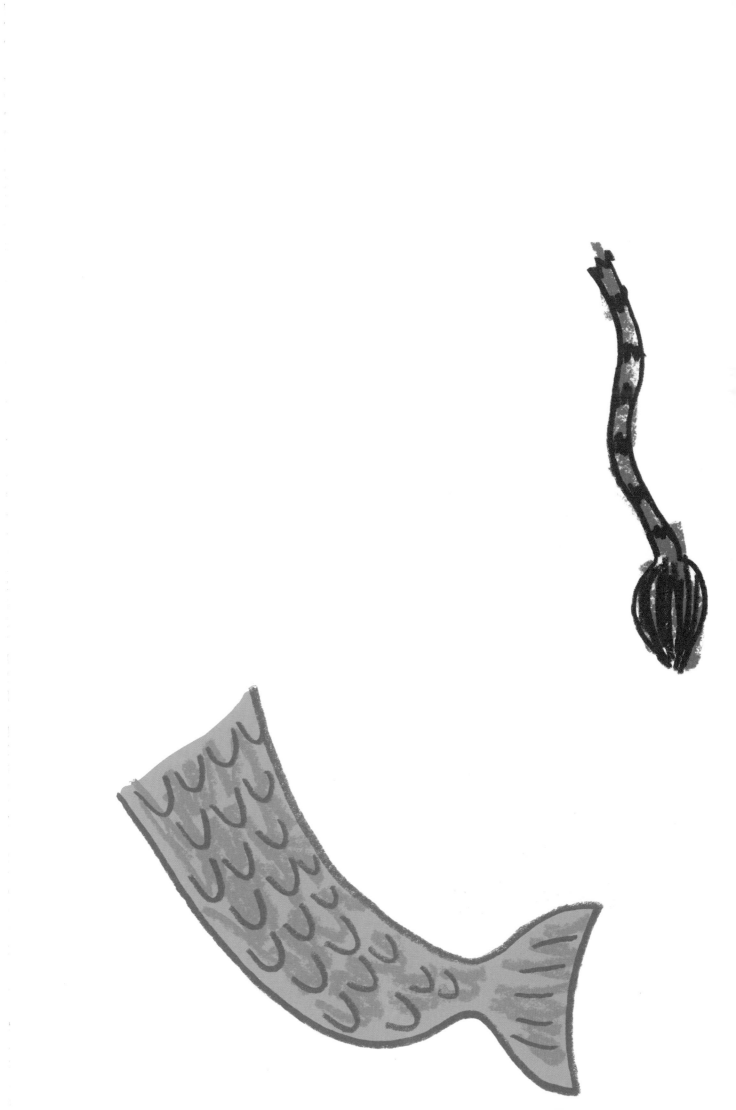

It breathes fire!

Whose shadows are these?

Mice or elephants?

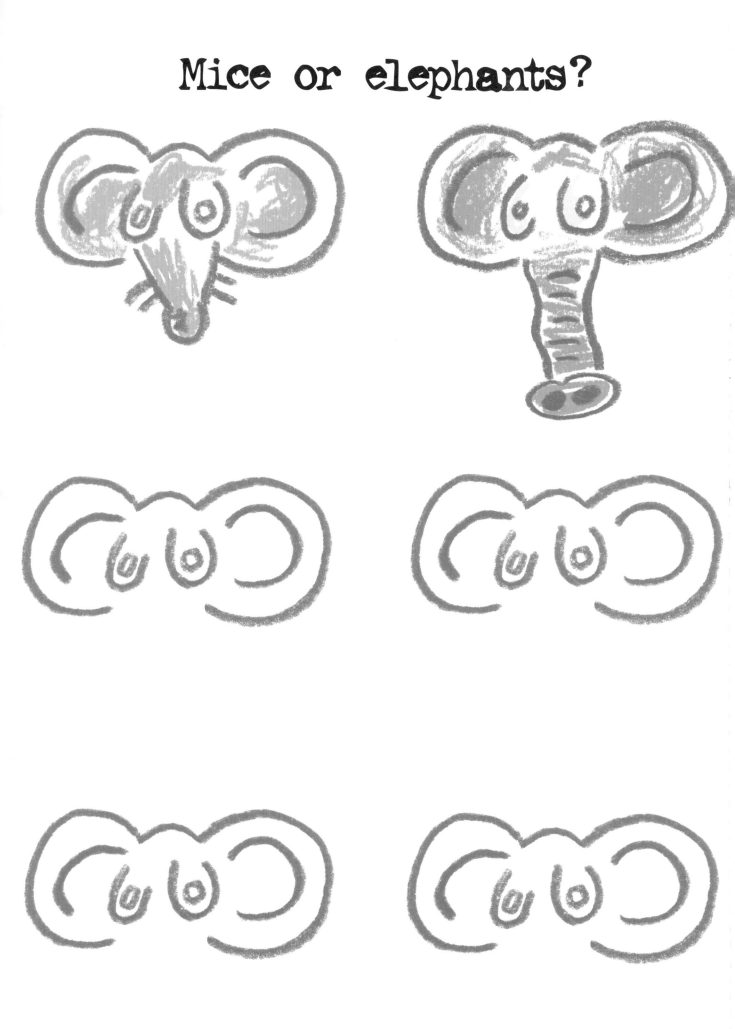

Achoo!

What's he shouting at?

What came crashing in?

What is jumping through the hoop?

Park the cars.

I spy with my little eye
something beginning with S.

Who's in the elevator?

What's carrying me away?

What's in my
handkerchief?

Make it summer.

Shake the snow globe.

Trick or treat?

Who's on the bottom?

Fill the hat shop.

Win the tug-of-war.

What's that in your ear?

What's up my nose?

Germs...

What's in the rock pool?

What's in my pocket?

Make it stormy.

What's being transported?

What a view!

Squeeze it.

Open the umbrellas.

Nits...

Round things...

What happened?

What's in the safe?

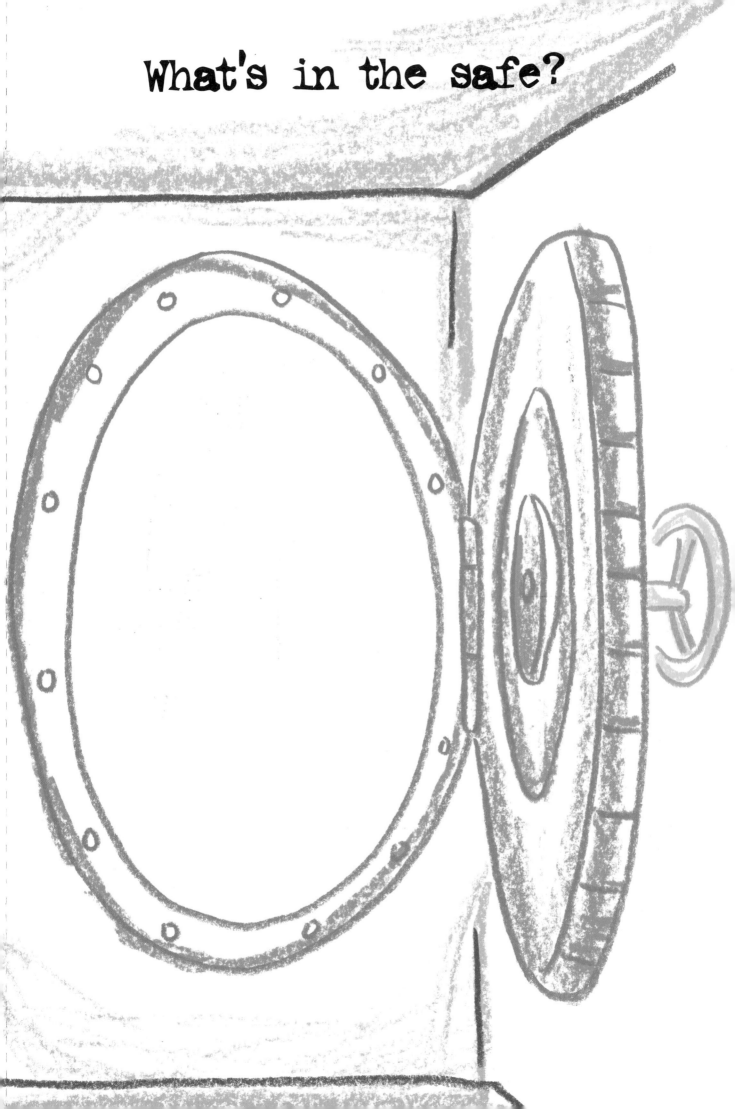

Whose home?

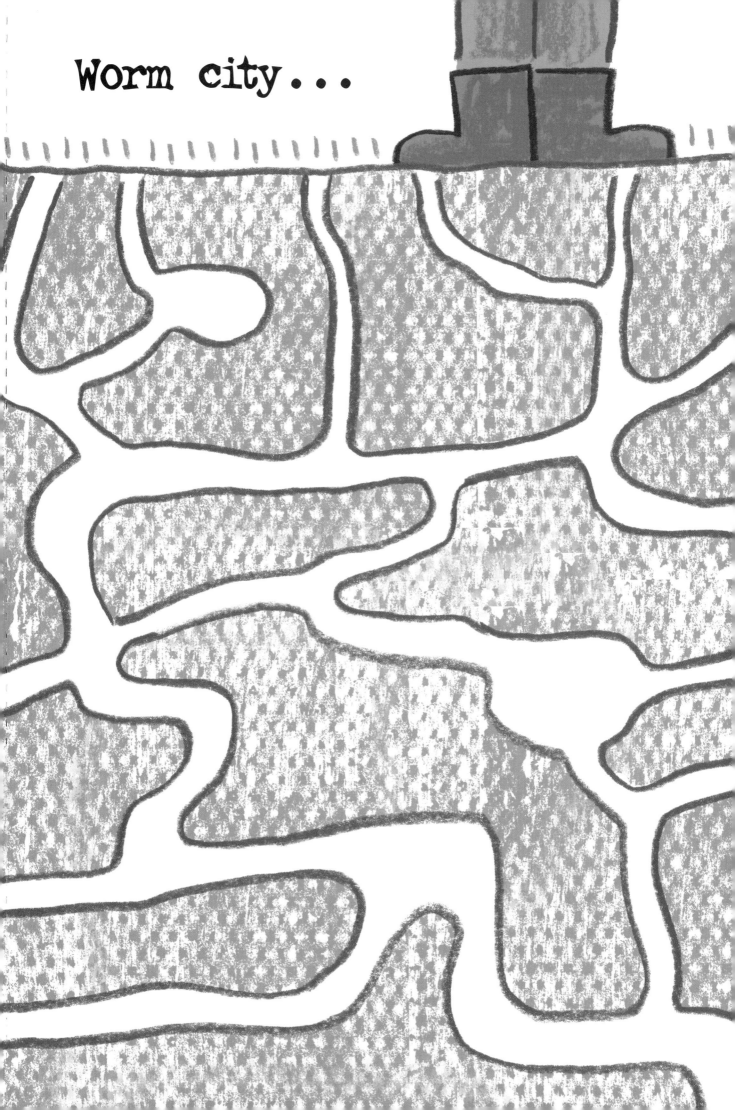

Worm city...

Sheep or trees?

I spy with my little eye something beginning with E.

Give the octopus legs.

Bury some treasure.

A room full of danger.

A room full of fun.

Whose footprints are these?

Fill the potions cupboard.